Ms. Murphy Fights Fires

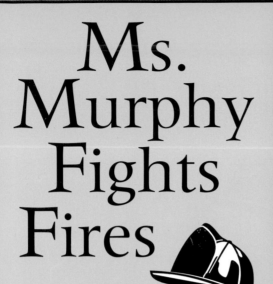

written by
ALICE K. FLANAGAN

photographs by
CHRISTINE OSINSKI

Reading Consultant
LINDA CORNWELL
Learning Resource Consultant
Indiana Department of Education

CHILDREN'S PRESS®   *A Division of Grolier Publishing*
New York • London • Hong Kong • Sydney • Danbury, Connecticut

Special thanks to Firefighter Judith Murphy-Beyar of Fire Engine Co. 152 for allowing us to tell her story.

Also, thanks to Fire Engine Co. 152, especially members:

FF. Anthony Lordo
FF. Steven Zasa
FF. Paul Coulbourne
FF. Leonard Yourth
FDNY Audiovisual Unit—FF. Booker
FDNY Forensic Unit—Lt. Smiouskas
FDNY Training Academy

Library of Congress Cataloging-in-Publication Data
Flanagan, Alice.
      Ms. Murphy fights fires / written by Alice K. Flanagan ; photographs by Christine Osinski ; reading consultant, Linda Cornwell.
        p. cm. — (Our neighborhood)
      Summary: Simple text and photographs follow a female firefighter as she and the rest of a fire-fighting team try to save a burning building.
      ISBN 0-516-20494-7 (lib.bdg.)   0-516-26212-2 (pbk.)
      1. Fire extinction—Juvenile literature. [1. Fire fighters. 2. Fire extinction. 3. Occupations.] I. Osinski, Christine, ill. II. Title. III. Series: Our neighborhood.
TH9148.F495 1997
628.9'25—dc21   97-2181
                                                            CIP
                                                             AC

Photographs ©: Christine Osinski

Smell the smoke?
Hear the fire alarm ring?
Somewhere, there is a fire!

At the firehouse, Ms. Murphy and the other firefighters answer the alarm when it comes in.

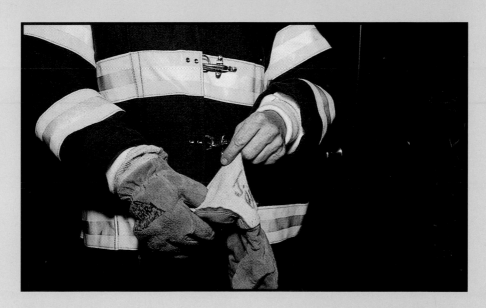

Ms. Murphy puts on special clothes to protect her from the smoke and heat. Then she rushes to the fire.

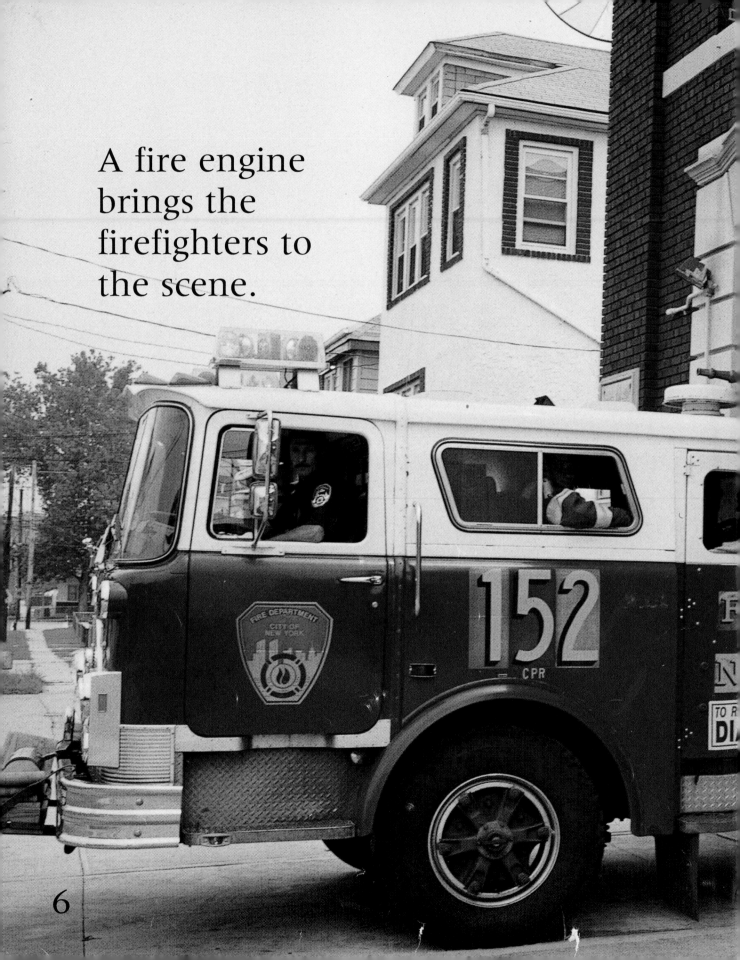

A fire engine
brings the
firefighters to
the scene.

6

The firefighters always work
together as a team to put out fires
and save lives.

At the fire, everyone has a job to do.

Sometimes, Firefighter Murphy
drives the fire engine to the fire
and stays with the truck.

She starts the pumps and makes sure
there is enough water in the hoses
to put out the fire.

Sometimes, she works in the burning building.

She climbs a ladder . . .

. . . and breaks down doors and windows when she can't get in.

Inside the building, it's dark and dangerous.

Firefighter Murphy wears a special mask so she can breathe fresh air.

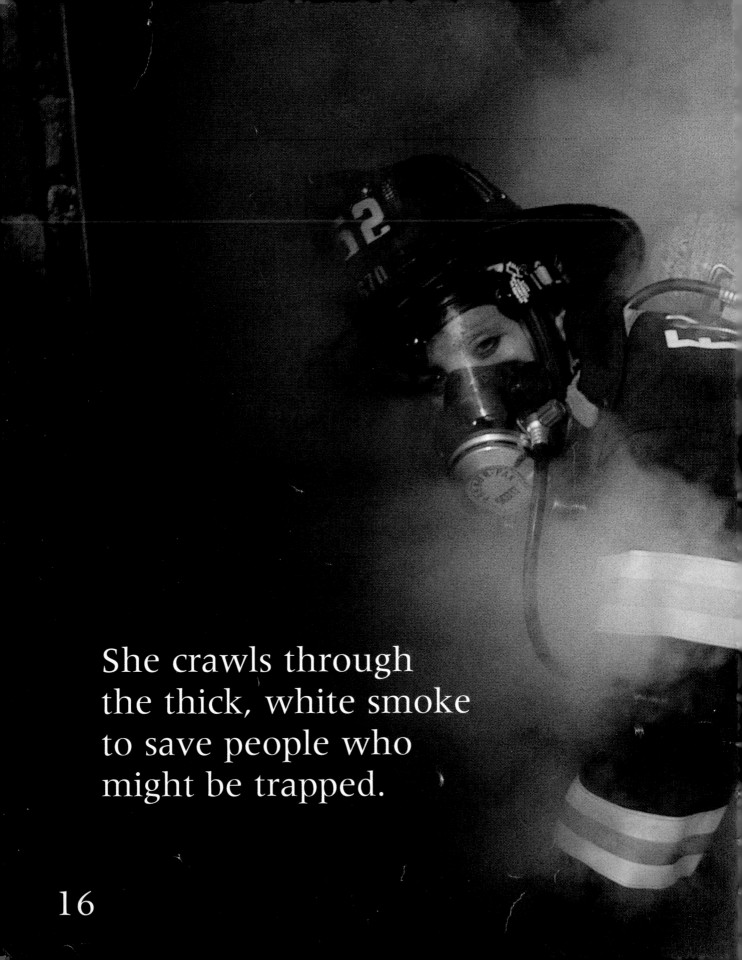

She crawls through
the thick, white smoke
to save people who
might be trapped.

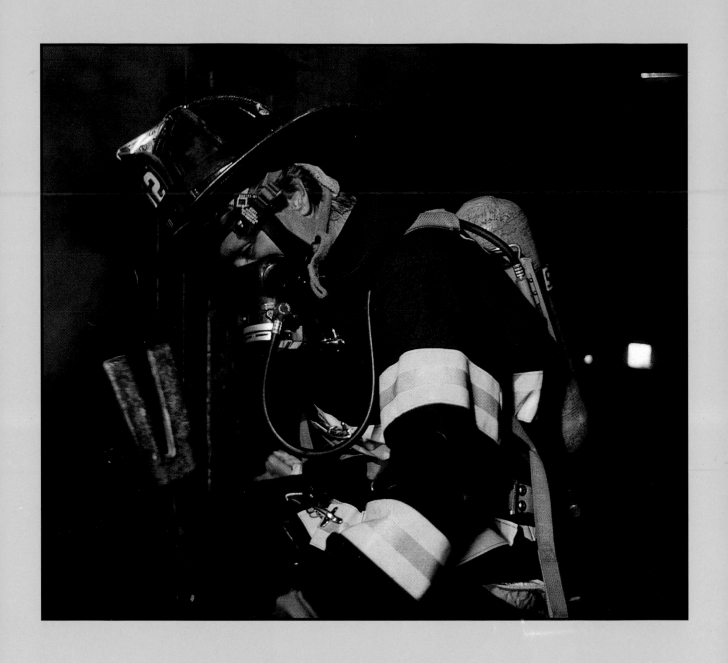

Firefighter Murphy must be careful.
The heat and flames can burn
everything in minutes.

She finds no people in the burning house. It's only an empty building.

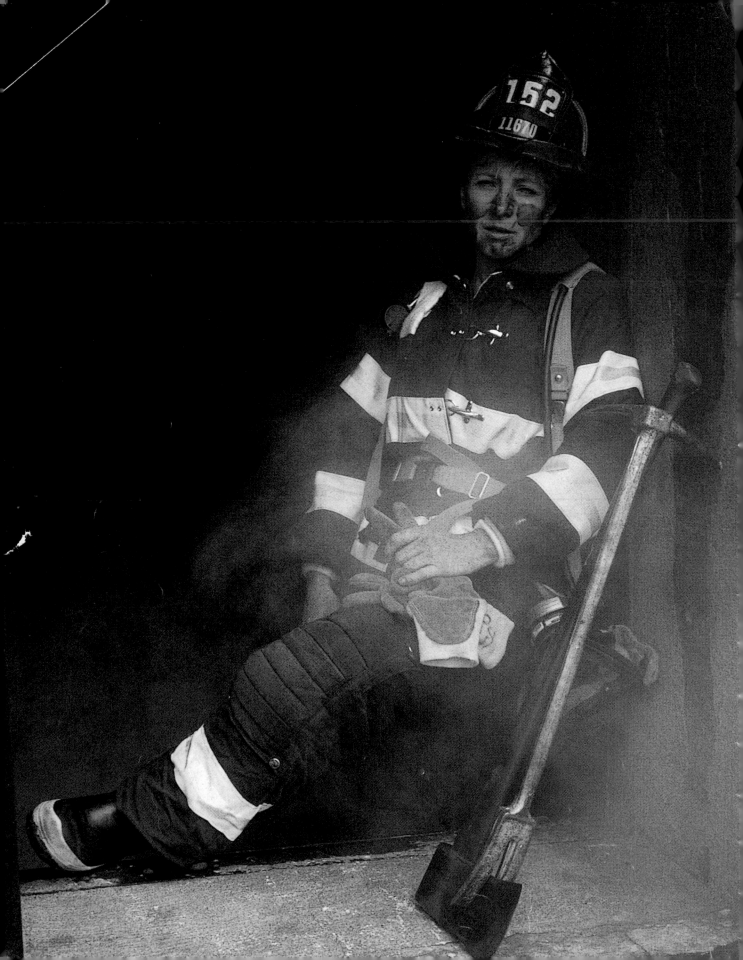

After the fire is out, a tired
Ms. Murphy and her team go home.

As a firefighter, Ms. Murphy does more than put out fires. She takes care of emergencies in the neighborhood.

When people come to the firehouse for help, Ms. Murphy knows what to do for them.

Ms. Murphy worked hard to become a firefighter.

Some people thought it was a job only men could do. She proved that they were wrong.

Ms. Murphy never gave up on her dreams. She believed she could be whatever she wanted to be.

Now she wants her three daughters, Alaina, Carly, and Julie, to have a chance to be whatever they want to be, too.

Ms. Murphy is a good mother and a brave firefighter.

She risks her life to help others. Some people call Ms. Murphy a saving angel.

Meet the Author
and the Photographer

Alice Flanagan and Christine Osinski are sisters. They grew up together telling stories and drawing pictures in a brown brick bungalow in a southwest-side neighborhood of Chicago, Illinois. Today they write stories and take photographs professionally.

Ms. Flanagan resides in Chicago with her husband and works as a freelance writer. Ms. Osinski is a photographer and teaches at The Cooper Union for the Advancement of Science and Art in New York City. She lives with her husband and two sons on Staten Island.